PRAISE FOR JIMMY BACA

"[Baca's poetry is] a powerful orchestration . . . with an utterly compelling dramatic form."

—LIAM RECTOR, *The Hudson Review*

"Jimmy Santiago Baca is a force in American poetry. . . . His words heal, inspire, and elicit the earthly response of love."

—GARRETT HONGO, Pulitzer Prize–nominated author of *The River of Heaven*

"Baca sings of the kind of hope only a courageous spirit can vision out of time and places which would crush most dreamers. If there is any North American poet who might wear the mantle of Pablo Neruda, it is Jimmy Santiago Baca."

—JOSEPH BRUCHAC, Native American storyteller

"We share in Baca's transcendence and are grateful."

—*The Bloomsbury Review*

"Baca has the ability to convey much in few words, and his precise use of detail delivers small, startling truths."

—*Publishers Weekly*

When I Walk
Through
That Door,
I Am

When I Walk Through That Door, I Am

An Immigrant Mother's Quest

JIMMY SANTIAGO BACA

Beacon Press
BOSTON

BEACON PRESS
Boston, Massachusetts
www.beacon.org

Beacon Press books
are published under the auspices of
the Unitarian Universalist Association of Congregations.

22 21 20 19   8 7 6 5 4 3 2 1

This book is printed on acid-free paper that meets the
uncoated paper ANSI/NISO specifications for
permanence as revised in 1992.

Text design and composition by Kim Arney

Library of Congress Cataloging-in-Publication Data

Names: Baca, Jimmy Santiago, author.
Title: When I walk through that door, I am : an immigrant
mother's quest / Jimmy Santiago Baca.
Description: Boston : Beacon Press, [2019]
Identifiers: LCCN 2018043630 (print) | LCCN 2018046864 (ebook) |
ISBN 9780807059470 (ebook) | ISBN 9780807059357 (pbk. : alk. paper)
Classification: LCC PS3552.A254 (ebook) |
LCC PS3552.A254 W48 2019 (print) |
DDC 811/.54—dc23

I dedicate this book to my wife, Stacy, and my kids, Lucia, Esai, Gabe, and Tones. Without them, I probably wouldn't be alive. And to Sae-Po, who enriched my life, and all the immigrants in the US who continue to struggle for a better life. I welcome you all, you who have built America and make it better by your presence, ever aspiring to create an even more just and equitable society for tomorrow. Without your spirit and heart and labor, indeed without your constant struggle for freedom and dignity, we would not enjoy the democratic values we do today. Thank you for your sacrifice and for making our freedom possible and for so much more. Your presence reminds us all what America is really about

CONTENTS

When I Walk
Through
That Door,
I Am

PART I

In San Salvador,
Tonal (my marido) works
night shift knitting clothing for export.
Gangs tax the workers half their check
but Tonal refuses to pay—we have a four
year old, Joaquin, but they don't care.

On Tonal's way home last night
4:30
in bed

                when I hear

angry voices outside
YOU PAY OR DIE
wheels screech
door slams
Tonal's voice begs for mercy

                    then

shots
boom! boom!

                    the car squeals off

leaving

Tonal's jagged voice
Sophia! . . . ayudame . . . ayudame . . . Sophia!

I rush from the bedroom
draw my yarn blanket and slippers on
(llama and sheep wool
Tonal made for me
on our 5th anniversary).

I dash into the night,
across the street
collapse next to Tonal
kneeling under the streetlight
in the neighbor's stone-dirt driveway.

I cradle Tonal's
body on my lap—
"Mi amor, mi amor!" I weep
as blood pools in the dirt
I tug his arm,

                    "Mi amor, mi amor!
                    No te mueres!" He groans,

> "Corre `pal Norte mi reina,
> con mejito, vete mi amor
> corre! o te matan!"

I scream, "Stay awake, stay awake!"

Blood surfs from his thighs
ladles out
from kneecaps
that look like potato peelings
on the cutting board.

The stones and dirt witness
The stones ask
The stones take
The stones tell
Lay on us, they whisper,
We will absorb your sadness.

Tonal died, me and my baby Joaquin
go North, `pal Norte, as he wanted,
to escape the wrath of the gangs.

At every port and border,
we encounter vigilantes,
uniformed official administrators
and unruly mobs,
shouting the same refrain,
"Go back to your country!"
and from American language radios
at the Mercado and from windows
talk-show celebrities
label us rebellious outlaws
criminals and drug dealers,
answering our misery
with four-walled thinking
(walls I vow to smash down one day,
an aloof and solitary woman
with mountain cliff fire
burning in me, burning in me).

The experts claim not to know
our oppression,
how we are tortured and murdered
and turned away at every door,
instead of the real people that we are—

hungry, kind, hard-working,
dreaming of an education and peaceful life,
their ideas replace us with stereotypes
that suit their selfish needs.

We did nothing wrong.

The shooting has taken the center
out of me,
leaves cartridges of shotgun shells
where my heart used to be,
in the center of me, smoldering,
how Tonal was on his way home
from work,
paper lunch sack clutched in hand,
San Martin De Porras medal around his neck
a turquoise-silver wedding band
his tio Tomas, a Huichol silversmith, made for us,
a heart tattoo with our names in it on his chest,
and *Joaquin*, *siempre mi amor*, on his left forearm.

I pack what I can carry and flee `pal Norte,
(I believe my husband's words,

believe them with my whole heart).
Joaquin strapped to my back,
four times jump trains as they are moving,
four times gang-raped
by predators and the police,
and as each man mounts me, a voice
in me speaks,
"*Will you tell them, hell is not a dream
and that you've been there, will you tell them?*"

And I whisper, *I will*.

In El Paso, Tx., I plead for asylum,
they bus me to the
Otero County Processing Center,
Immigration Detention Center
in Otero County, New Mexico
and ICE authorities take my baby Joaquin
and I am placed in a cell
and two ICE officials
rape me that night,
their glossy badges and pistols and leather belts
shimmering under the fluorescent ceiling lights,

their sweat and tongue-flickering spit
sprinkles my cheeks and forehead,
veins pulse at their necks
reddened faces
swollen and eyes glazed angry
sparkle with madness.

The Cibola County Correctional Center
run by CoreCivic in Otero County,
is a machine that turns its cruel amusement-wheels
manufacturing manufacturing manufacturing
packaged lies that I am a worthless villain—

(I want to be me, who I am inside myself,
back to myself, blessed with awareness,
vulnerable, gentle with myself and others,
hope that one day I might be able to live again.)

I am raped
by an ICE officer again,
he grunts and squeals like a pink pig, and
the stones and dirt witness
The stones ask

The stones take
The stones tell
Lay on us,
We will absorb your sadness.

I close my eyes, vowing never
to become a prison company-whore for favors—
cokes, chips and cigarettes.

I close my eyes and see Tonal
hovering in the air around me.
"She's bleeding," I hear an ICE officer's voice say
to his partner on top of me, who replies,
"What she gonna do, call 911?" He laughs,
"Let the bitch die, the more that do
the better off we are."

Tonal and Joaquin's bright eyes grow
with blinding sunshine over me,
burning away their smell and touch and laughter,
burning away the gunshots that killed Tonal
that still shudder my dreams with snarls

and scare me,

 burning away

gangs, clubs, bombs, body parts
strewn in the streets, paramilitary death squads
that scare me,

 burning away

patriotism's blood-hunger
that devours, maims, silences Salvador's children—
a Democracy that stalks us
and roams the dark land of our sorrow
smothered in flames and blood of our loved ones—

The stones and dirt witness
The stones ask
The stones take
The stones tell
Lay on us,
We will absorb your sadness.

Tonal and Joaquin's eyes shine like the sun,
as if to say, Mama, healing
is the word for *challenge,*

is another word
to dream what is possible—

they convey
looking into my brown eyes
all of us,
who journeyed
undocumented
from cosmic
sunlit
regions of the universe

into earthlings
with hands, mouth, lips
breast, ears, toes, hips . . .

like all of us
once a child
filled with questions—

Mother, what is that,
his first sensual exploration into
the world

spark't light in his heart
brimmed
seeds
of his origin-ness,
what is that
and I say a chili pepper
and in the bell tower
I say a pigeon
and dirt between fingers
I say sandbox soil
and that
feeling my lips on his cheek
I say a kiss
    and
    when he kisses me
    I ask
    what is that
    he says love.

———

Now they have Joaquin caged somewhere
and I listen to the rumors

from other women: they sell the children
to sex traffickers,
use them for forced child labor,
sell them to wealthy white people . . .

In San Salvador, the night of the shooting,
I pleaded with La Policia
to at least call an ambulance,
pero respondio, " Pa que gastar tiempo y feria, son animales . . ."

That morning
September lawns and bare trees
studied the crime scene
to understand what imbues
the dawn with sorrow
darkening it
with the feeling that it is
harder to have hope—
that the violence will never end.

Me voy al Norte,
Joaquin beside me
we walk for weeks through the foothills,

where my heart flares its nostrils
quivering, puffing,
as cacti and hundred-year-old cedars
root in desert granite crevices
counsel me in patience.

The stones and dirt witness
The stones ask
The stones take
The stones tell
Lay on us,
We will absorb your sadness.

I have an overwhelming need
to sit on a boulder and weep
for my marido, for me, my `jito, Joaquin—
so many children in San Salvador
line the cemetery rows,
so many funerals daily!

I held my marido's head in my lap
breathed on his face
it was going to be alright,

my face under the streetlight
smooth as the jade plant,
my voice
wind chimes
declaring my love to him forever.

———

Tonal came to me last night
in fragments of a dream:
our life together once—
me in the garden planting chili peppers,
him cutting and nailing boards for the herbs,
Joaquin jumping on the trampoline—
illuminated red hot in my dream
like jagged asteroids
that flew through space
in my sleep,
warm tortillas
that nourish my heart
for the journey.

And then I dream of Joaquin
bits and pieces of a dream—

I am in the woods, at the sea,
atop a mountain,
opening my arms to embrace all of them
with the growl of a jaguar!

They fly toward me from outer space
as if I am the center
their destination
their homeland, shattered,

            now return

to create

            a new life.

————

            At night,
            while women in the dorm
            crowd around the radio
            to hear news
            of their disappeared children . . .

surf stations
with hosts accusing refugees
of carrying disease and infections,
of being terrorists and drug addicts,

young ones, 14, 15, 16 year olds
drugged by doctors
and counselors working for ICE,
are taken out to drink and party
and return at dawn,
with new shoes, blouses and bracelets.

————

At the prison fence this morning
I stand and feed a roadrunner:
the only desert bird who taunts the rattler,
luring it forth, expands its umbrella wings, idling
inches from it when the snake whip-lunges at it,
and the roadrunner fakes in
skips back from the venomous fangs,
hops clear
until it snatches the snake up with its beak,
smashes its head against a stone
and swallows it whole.

Sleek gray shield of feathers,
black spots and white edgings

swoops in a single blink-of-an-eye
on brick walls, over bushes, across the patrol path
fast and agile as a super-sized hummingbird—
I toss cooking pot scraps
and dinner greens (given me by the kitchen help)
on the grass,
he eats tame as any yard dog.

I pray for the roadrunner
to check on my four-year-old Joaquin,
now classified a criminal
by the United States,
guard him against the snakes.

I tell the stones
he was a pre-school child once
racketing hallways clacking his skates
in his cubby,
hanging his rain slicker on wooden pegs
and stamping in rain puddles with his galoshes.

He grew wings
at recess

when the bell rang
scudded back
his desk,
anxious to fly over
the playground
perch on the merry-go-round
like a quetzal in the rainforest.

His heart's door hinges
grimaced
with the coming and going
of so much happiness through him,
as he raced others
to hopscotch
under the shed
or soccer on the courts,
dangled on monkey bars
and yelped down dented slides.

At the fence on another morning
I am startled and shriek a serrated cry
and other women rush out, thinking

the worst—I had broken a bone, been shot,
but instead, what happened, a hawk
landed on the fence bar
perched a few feet from my face
and studied me for minutes—
a moment with no beginning or end,
an infinite meeting of two travelers;
in the hawk's eyes all it had seen—
desert, forest, seas, fields, cliffs,
and because when I was a child I lived in the rainforest
bathed myself in mud-pits used by Huichol ancestors
plastering mud on my small body—

                    the hawk knew me

as it knows a tree or the air beneath its wings
and gave me in that moment all the lands it had soared over,

                    leaving me a feather

that had brushed against the sun.

———————

I placed candles and flowers
where Tonal was murdered,

the owner of the house
within the hour of his murder
had already hosed the blood away,
had a contractor with them
on their plan to install a wall
rimmed with razor wire
to keep predators from climbing over.

This is the ritual for senseless death:
to remove flowers and candles
and hose away the blood,
as if it never happened,
reducing the value of life to nothingness.

———————

A new busload of ICE agents arrive
and as the morning hour makes its rounds
like a green-uniformed jailer,
the bus filled with young recruits,
stare out the window with pale faces
as if they are prisoners serving
a sentence for a crime of indifference.

They don't see
Democracy's body
on the barbwire,
a mangled prisoner
trying to escape its torturers. . . .

————

Ay Tonal,
my despair
is the saw-tooth chain that cuts through bone,
its growl roars through my heart
scattering bone-dust
and what was once anger
is reduced to a stump,
cut down into sizes
that fit my heart's black-iron stove;
I kneel on the floor in front of my heart
shove my despair in, watch
the flames engulf it,
the fire flows in blind reverence
allowing no exit

                    nor escape

for my despair
as its reckoning
turns all to ash.

And when the fires of despair burn down
and darkness fills me
I no longer know how
to find my way out under the moon and stars:
my child
cries for me to take his hand and lead him
                    out of the dark house,
                    for me
to say, it's ok, the terror will go and things
will get better.

I pray,
I get the red gasoline can and fill the chainsaw,
check the oil,
sharpen each claw on the chain with a file
until the ridge-teeth gleam
                    cold as a blade
and keep chopping my anger up
feeding it to the fire.

———

I walk the compound yard
carrying you in my thoughts
I feel like I am walking up a mountain
meditating on you my sweet Joaquin,
where are you? are you safe? do you have nightmares?
do you cry at night, are you eating, are you sick?

I keep walking
carrying you in my thoughts
I feel I am walking up a mountain
I feel the exertion
of my breath and my lungs
feel alive
I stop to catch my breath
I turn around and I realize
I can see so much further
than just what's in front of me
I can see all around.

I keep walking
carrying you in my thoughts

I feel I am walking up a mountain
and say to myself, damn,
feeling the mountain
pull my strength from me
it reels in my stamina,
I stand and breathe for a while
the way a fish poises mid water in a stream
still and one with the water,
so I am with the mountain I climb.
For mothers like me, climbing a mountain
is sometimes the only cure.

I keep walking
carrying you in my thoughts
I feel I am walking up a mountain
there's something really wonderful
at the end of my walk, I'm exhausted
my cheeks numb,
I don't have the strength for anything
and I look around and appreciate where I landed:
after being raped by American officials,
after being robbed by gangs and crossing borders,

after broken families and arguing and fighting
I get to the place
where I'm numb
from the goodness of the boulders and pines and
    streams,
from roaming the mountains and standing under
    the trees
and red stone cliffs and sandstone buttes and mesas,
thousands of years old,
I feel my heart is as old and wise
and I keep walking
carrying you in my thoughts, Joaquin,
I feel I am walking up a mountain
having taken my place
among nature where you've always wanted to be
a place you've worked to get to
and the pay-off is not money nor fame
but feeling yourself alive.

I keep walking
carrying you in my thoughts
I feel I am walking up a mountain

I keep climbing and breathing hard
to get a lifetime of betrayals out,
climb and breathe hard, huff, groan, pant, grunt out
through my nose and mouth, hefty exhales and sighs,
until I blow out and whew! a dozen times
and start climbing again
and bow to the earth for the wounds
from those I thought were trustworthy allies.

I keep walking
carrying you in my thoughts
I feel I am walking up a mountain
my legs do not betray me
when I walk up the steep hills
every footstep in the dirt
opens a door, affirms your existence,
your rounded presence in the fallen leaves
that stick to the twigs like small ancient hands
sink back into earth to stir roots, water and seeds
to serve in Spring the gruel of flowers and field grasses.

I keep walking
carrying you in my thoughts

I feel I am walking up a mountain
think of all the poisons and haters
that have filled you and come at you
on any ordinary day
and see how the hill gently rises and lifts itself up
in defiance and joy of being itself—
the steepest hills as my legs and calves and knees
hurt but see how the sun manages to shine
through every space available to it as you do for me my son.
Stones and branches and trees in your way
make a beautiful definition of your self
you shine through.

I keep walking
carrying you in my thoughts
I feel I am walking up a mountain,
come my son
let your heart be as the cactus
with its spikes
protruding from the crusty dirt
offer the world your bouquet of thorns,
your heart reddens the dirt
when you touch the world.

Walk more, walk with me Joaquin,
let your lungs acclimate to the air
until your body begins its quiet song
without singing without words
moving in tune to the silence of the land
as you grieve a sweet sadness of missing your mother,
for how badly the world treated you.

I keep walking
carrying you in my thoughts
I feel I am walking up a mountain
see the old black cedars
that have lived for 500 years
decaying in their own glory
like candle wicks on a chapel altar
slowly smolder back
to their dark grief
let your grief be as such my son,
burn bright your grief before all the saints.

They say if you pick a grain from an anthill
put it under your tongue
ants will carry your dream

to the place where it comes true
and then return it on their backs, to you.
My whole mouth is an anthill.

You who have had
a hard time living around hostile people
look up my son
stand between two pines of your father and me
and with your heart wish all your enemies a good journey—

you don't need to go to another place
stand amongst pines and listen to the wind
know you are the flame the wind cannot blow out
the more the wind talks the higher you become
and in a quiet way I will keep on walking,
with each footstep, feeling you
more and more as you want to be
I will keep walking
carrying you in my thoughts
I feel I am walking up a mountain.

———

The stones and dirt witness
The stones ask
The stones take
The stones tell
Lay on us,
We will absorb your sadness.

———

On November 8th
I return from the kitchen
to find Ursula my cellmate weeping—
I kneel down before the desk she sits at
and ask what happened
and she tells me,
bottom lip quivering, trying with all her might to
    stop crying
so she can speak,
"My sister called, they got him, the gangs, killed him!"

On her bunk are newspaper clippings:

" . . . To maximize their criminal profits, these human smugglers crammed more than 100 people into a tractor trailer in the stifling Texas summer heat resulting in ten dead and 29 others hospitalized."

And, from an interview with a journalist,

"With all the drug wars and daily killings, it's a war zone here, military jeeps and guns and helicopters everywhere and I just read this morning that the Supreme Court has ruled that high-ranking federal officials in your country cannot be held responsible for abuse against individuals held in prisons and detention centers, even when that abuse results from their policies and directives. I have interviewed dozens of Central Americans who have been tortured in the American prison system.

Line up the coffins of immigrants murdered trying to cross the border and they would stretch from coast to coast— Pacific to Atlantic: they're not arresting the slave-traders, bandits and drug dealers— hundreds of bodies of women, children and men die from dehydration and predators every month.

What strategy is this? Genocide? A Mexican–Central American holocaust? Most are fleeing civil wars, gangs, cartels, others are starving, want to work but the borderlands have become a death-camp for them."

On November 1st, at approximately 3 AM, Ursula's husband's body was found on the Pinotepa highway. He was intercepted by two trucks containing armed individuals. He was then tortured, assaulted and left tied and naked, his tongue cut out and fingers broken.

———

I felt nauseous—something was happening that was changing my life forever.

Ursula hung herself while I was sleeping. I was a friend of Ursula's, we walked together.

Her death brings up memories.

> Tonal, your death,
> touches my heart each day

like the tires of a plane on the runway crashing
it jolts my heart hard enough
so my heart cracks as if it is old and dry.

It's been over a year since the Cartel
and Federales murdered you.
It's hard to face the truth about your absence
but I learn how to see life through the lens of
      your death,
the lens of bigotry, racism, the stagnant, lynch-
      mentality media
that pours like raw sewage from TVs
until I am so fatigued with violence,
I can hardly stir at the news that a family of eight,
six children and parents all murdered, mutilated,
beheaded, skinned alive by para-military
      right wingers
almost humdrum business as usual.

———————

The president is visiting us today
followed by an army of reporters

to show Americans this is not a concentration camp
that we are happy campers, not prisoners.

I stand by the barbwire fence
biting into a peach
I suck and roll the pit on my tongue
around in my mouth
as juice runs over my lips.

The sweet juice uncurls its
exuberance for being alive
reaching out with compassion and kindness in me.

For days, the Secret Service have been setting up
        on rooftops,
linesmen on the telephone poles
install surveillance cameras,
everyone is being watched.
                    Armed ICE assassins
                    stand at the wall,
other security men
tied up with ropes and links and cleat-boots
        stand ready for assault, talk into their earpiece devices.

If urged to talk on camera to America
I would ask
that you open the door,
invite us to your table,
welcome and respect
and help and appreciate us,
because that is what we did
when you called on us
to feed you, to shelter you,
to clothe and protect you,
when Settlers from the West
came upon our shores
lost and afraid and sick,
we warmed you at our fires,
bedded you in warm blankets,
healed you, cured you,
cared for your children—
open your heart,
as we did ours.

I ask in good faith
stop committing hate crimes
against us—

don't beat us as you have, don't starve
or deny us our loved ones,

       have goodwill toward us
don't darken our days with a wall
don't redden our clothing with our blood
don't shoot, stab, kick, bury or imprison us
as you do today,

       don't trade and buy and sell
       our children,
as if we are not human.

I am an immigrant mother on a quest for freedom.
There is no retreat.

Show me,
kindness, compassion, understanding,
many of us have died
have been murdered,
have been abused, slaughtered, burned,
lynched, attacked;

practice your humanity,
drop your racism, shed your bigotry,

show good will to me
stop persecuting me,
stop hating
stop—
be just, obey the law, respect my right
to live,
we are 40 million strong in America,
40 million who love Democracy
unapologetically.

———————

Before lights-out, huddled on bunks,
we worry as we listen to women read their letters and talk:

*"Agents swept through the International District here,
targeting large numbers of women and children, dragging
them out of schools. On my way to work I'm followed by
ICE agents. They arrested 160 at the poultry plant and even
people with work permits are getting arrested."*

*And, "I've filed for asylum for you, the cartels threatened you
because of what you've written. As a journalist, you have*

to be protected or stop writing and since you won't stop, you have to come here. Your cousin can get you on the shoe factory until you get a job at a newspaper."

And, "*Mi Querida Clementina,* I went to a rally on the International Bridge this afternoon, hundreds of people protesting the immigration policy. It was encouraging but sad as some were led off in shackles around their ankles, wrists, and waist. Doing my part, I threw small pumpkins at the ICE agents. Pumpkins or watermelons, nothing seems to stop these people who behave like Gestapos and so I drove to church, maybe praying will help. In the middle of the night flashing red lights wake us—the drug war murders continue and while I hear machine guns blasting away, I curl up on the couch and watch Netflix and forget about my miserable life for an hour.

"Migrants the world over are dying as people watch like sports fans the grim spectacle of fishing trawlers recover the hundreds of bodies. Enough bodies to fill an airplane hangar. People assuage their guilt with teddy bears and roses, every living room and bedroom and yard and kitchen

*should be filled with mourners, public opinion no longer
matters—at least not in Mexico, where every nine out of
ten government official is corrupt—the higher you go, the
more corruption.*

*"But there are a few brave men and women working to destroy
Mafia & Cartel networks—if I were to really write what I
felt I'd say behead the bosses, burn the boats, tractor trailers and
planes, burn their mansions and luxury cars and money and
let the burning be our anthem that returns us to our humanity,
enough assassinations and killing journalists, prosecutors,
judges, police officers, and politicians, no more submission to
organized crime, tens of millions of people flee war, starvation,
and oppression while for those living in transit countries—the
drivers, the fixers, the translators, the guards, the shopkeepers,
the brokers, the bookkeepers, the police officers, the checkpoint
runners, the bandits—business has never been more profitable
for them."*

And, *"Shooting Asylum-Seekers has its own season with the
dead hanging from trees while profit margins widen and
gun profiteers become wealthier."*

———————

I witness the slow burn
of San Salvador's dying Democracy—
you contain me as if I was nuclear waste
in an underground tomb,
you mistrust me as if I was an enemy
in a cold war,
you isolate me from my son,
you strip me of all comforts
and terrorize me—

there they come,
wrapped in expensive scarves, carrying
briefcases, red ties, white starched shirts,
blue tailored suits, fresh from wine gatherings,
fresh from saunas and gyms and department Mall stores,
laughing, filing past the uniformed guards
posted along the walkway,
protecting the black garbed supreme court
judges, in bulletproof black limos
congressmen, senators,
talk-show heads and correspondents

military guards salute,
the red carpet stretched out, the door swings open
and out strut the powerful—

the motorcade snakes along,
White crowds scream and wave behind barricades,
and cannot with all their whiteness
light the long dark night of injustice
as they record on cameras,
rain slickered, poncho'd,
black-caped,
not even the rain can douse the burning
of our freedom on this day.

His visit backfired and all across the land
a hundred million Americans filled the streets—
demonstrations, protestors,
the poor, relatives of the murdered, the jailed,
    the unschooled,
homeless, even well-to-do and affluent people
marched and demanded justice
until they were forced to release us.

PART II

The day I am freed,
when I walk through the internment camp door I am Gandhi,
when I walk through the door I am Che,
(in my heart I say it louder now)
when I walk through the door
I throw my worries away, I let my frustrations go,
all ill-will I have for others I let go,
I brush my sleeves of the uncertainties of yesterday,
when I walk through that door
if someone should ask you
tell them I am Ali,
tell them I am Cesar Chavez,
when I walk through that door,
when I take a step forward, when I turn the corner
tell the world should they ask
I am who I dream myself to be—a scientist, a doctor,
a dancer, a poet, let the whole world know
I am who I dream myself,
(my heart cries louder and louder, with passion!)
tell them there goes the poet, there goes the painter,
tell all the haters and racists and cynics
I will not let them influence how I see myself,
that I am shaped by the loving hands of a dream,

no one makes me as they wish,
tell them please from conference halls and classrooms
from every street corner and market where you meet,
tell them you have seen me and talked to me
and that I am who I dream myself to be—
when I opened my eyes this morning
I surrendered to my greatness,
I knelt down
and opened my arms to embrace my full being,
my potential to be who I am in this world—
leader, teacher, activist, tell them I no longer am
the woman they knew, that I have
found a way to love myself—
I closed my eyes,
and when I opened them,
I know that when I walk through that door
I am
Mother Teresa, Zapata, Anzaldua, Betita, Sor Juana,
Celia Cruz, Menchu . . .
because the day is young and I've got mountains to move,
mountains to move.

My driver's name was Ben, in his eighties,
and Ben forgot where the highway was;
we found it and we headed toward Denver
and eight hours later
we passed the blue horse rearing
with front legs clawing the air
other-worldly, red fiery eyes
righteously heralding Armageddon;
while working on it in his studio in New Mexico,
it trampled him, crashing down on

    Jimenez (the sculptor)
and killed him;
for some it elicits a paranormal threat,
a satanic messenger of forthcoming destruction,
to others it carries a kind of presence
as if Jimenez' soul breathed inside its muscular body;
my attention was focused on its hooves
mane and nostrils and I wanted to hear it whinny
and gallop off across the prairie
neighing, "I will find your son."

Ten minutes from Denver, I ask Ben
where we are going and he doesn't know.

"I was just told to give you bus fare
and drop you off at the bus station."

——————

My traveling amiga's cousin Veronica
says they are hiring in Virginia
and when I arrive in Lexington, Va.,
    on Thursday, I am hired on the spot to be a maid:
clean the classrooms at Washington-Lee University
        prune the campus shrubs, and then I got a
            second job
at the Sheridan Livery Inn, in Lexington, Va.,
which used to be a stagecoach stop in 1887
and serviced the town with mail delivery and horse
        boarding,
within walking distance
is the Stonewall Jackson house and General Lee house
and museum on campus. I clean them all.

I get up an hour earlier than needed
take off on a walk

and listen to the chirping in treetops
see squirrels scamper
across composting mulch at the base of trees,
pigeons perched on Civil War hero statues
looming over the grassy stretches of rolling campus hills.
I shatter Stonewall Jackson & General Lee's
assumptions about me—
I am no one's slave, I am more beautiful
and creative and powerful than a million statues
I break down into shards with my feather duster.

I walk around the football field,
   I keep walking
   carrying you in my thoughts
   I feel I am walking up a mountain,
past the red-brick,
white colonnaded buildings
commanding over the campus lawns,
passing white retirees playing tennis,
white students racing past me,
the deep and shadowy forest
with a creek meandering through it

surrounding the school grounds,
where I find myself walking,

    I keep walking

    carrying you in my thoughts

    I feel I am walking up a mountain,
on the track walking in reverie,
unaware of the number of laps completed,
my mind absorbed by you my little dove

    I keep walking

    carrying you in my thoughts

    I feel I am walking up a mountain,
and then later, a poet named Seth, from Argentina,
took me to dine like a Conquistadora
at the Red Hen Restaurant
where chef, Matt Adams, cooked me lamb
from Shenandoah Lamb Co.
located in Lexington
where they bought the lamb whole
and broke it down in the kitchen,
my meal consisting of a trio—a braised leg,
a pan seared tenderloin and a crepinette,
which is a French style sausage patty
wrapped in caul fat and seared on both sides,

roasted in the oven
and everything was topped with grains of paradise
just made from the bones of the lamb.
It was served on top goat cheese couscous
and diced local bell peppers.
(It was the best meal of my life and I asked the chef
to write it all down for me!)

Later, Seth walks me to my apartment
and on the way there,
we are followed by ICE agents.
I tell him, "I am not afraid."
And I keep walking
            carrying you in my thoughts
            and I am not afraid anymore
(I am that horse
with front legs clawing the air
and other-worldly, red fiery eyes
righteously heralding Armageddon
as I look for my baby boy).

———

When emptying the trashcan in a classroom
I found this book written by a man named James Baldwin.
"You write in order to change the world, knowing
perfectly well that you probably can't . . . The world
changes according to the way people see it, and if you alter,
even by a millimeter, the way people look at reality, then
you can change it."

I walk around the football field,
          I keep walking
          carrying you in my thoughts
     I feel I am walking up a mountain,
     you are somewhere out there my son, my sweet Joaquin,
among the 41,300 people arrested for deportation in the
     last three months,
among the 11,000 who had no criminal convictions,
among the 2.3 million people in 1,719 state prisons,
     102 federal prisons,
942 juvenile correctional facilities, 3,283 local jails,
and 79 Indian Country jails as well as in military prisons,
immigration detention facilities, civil commitment centers,
     and prisons in the U.S. territories,
     you are out there mejito and I will find you.

And one day you will be here with me,
graduating,
whip-snapping on your skateboard,
ramping off a staircase handle railing
taking five-and-ten step leaps,
whirling the board beneath you with your feet
like a lion tamer's whip
and the tiger jumps through a hoop of fire
obeys
you as the board
turning the wheel coaster and board
this wild untamed thing
bringing it to life,
sweating, bruised, cut, hurt, broken
toes and swollen wrists, shoulders and cut knees,
sprained ankles,
burning with sweat and exhaustion
you go again and again
again and again
teaching me
a new world order
of love,
as if you were the morning sunlight,

spread your loving look into my heart's window,
spread over my room your infinite glow, a radiance
that creates hope
as I walk around the football field,

>I keep walking
>carrying you in my thoughts
>I feel I am walking up a mountain.

I will find you.

————

Diary Entry
August 7, 2018

My Son Joaquin:

I've been here almost a year and ICE tells me they still
can't find you.

World made of words, words put together to make
sense of the world. As a child of five I memorized
religious hymns, singing the loudest in the choir to hear
my voice and while the day emptied its classrooms I

spun like a globe on the teacher's desk, touching the sun as if it was a large alphabet card above the blackboard.

Mysteries—I was a wizard and with letter sounds I could conjure spells to chase the devil away, I could make stories up, poems, adventures, tragedies, romances, all at my disposal in my love for sharing wonderful fables the imagination called upon me to convey!

While grandpa buffed linoleum foyers, I sailed out of the present, touched paper as one touches a petal, scratched my fingernails on wooden desktops like a cub sharpening his claws on tree bark, ran my palm along the blackboard, unwadded crumpled papers in the wastebasket, then dashed out and slid down halls grandpa oiled with his dust mop.

In time, I memorized the card symbols, fingered letters in the yard dirt and welcomed the ant and cockroach into my world. I expanded my universe: I traced a letter on the cold window glass and everything about me shifted radically: I was reborn. Words de-created me and gave birth to a new me, I felt myself an alchemist's chalice filled with purposeful invention.

Even now as I write these words, images rise in the mist and slowly unveil what was hidden in the dawn fog: I see my hard-working grandma shaking her finger and scolding me no writing on everything—in the tortilla flour on the cutting board; in the dough; with my saliva beading on the hot woodstove top; when I peed outside in the dirt—don't do that! she cried, stop writing letters everywhere!

When they kidnapped you, words stopped working for me. More and more I realize I must do something for us, beyond waiting. Beyond hope. Beyond trusting what they say. For me, for others.

They should be testing the students on kidnappings, on racism, on injustice, test why a child cries for his mother, why a mother is sad and mourns for her stolen child, about a father who was murdered and doesn't come home, about a mother on drugs, about poverty, about fear, teach stories that talk about this, about never having enough to get by, about never being enough of a person to be accepted.

I work in this elitist university.

When I think of you, Joaquin, my soul unfolds, my heart opens. I look around the world and am saddened and troubled by the maddening violence, wars, quarrels, greed, insane power grabbers, the numbing of America and gargantuan greed of the rich.

My parents believed in books and words and when they spoke it was always with kindness. Thinking of you and them awakens a new part of myself and I trust this process that changes me, helps me also unclasp my tight-clenched fists and exhale and reach out to other hands that help me climb out of my darkness, as I lean toward the window in my soul and inhale the fresh air again, feeling clean, lighter, clearer of mind and heart and this helps me from being destroyed by what the Prison Profiteers have done to you and me, by what the Multi-National Corrections Industrial Complex that trades in criminalizing and destroying human beings and ruining our communities have done to us. May the spirit of my parents' kindness and your beauty Joaquin shape my speech so that I may continue to speak on your behalf, live on your behalf, and never give up searching for you.

Sae-Po (everything we know about them is wrong)

Unless Democracy is in the heart, it doesn't matter much how many documents are signed or piled up in shelves of libraries until the ceiling beams crack and columns collapse; it won't work. There's a lot of us, however, who do know and do practice the values we herald and defend in our Constitution, and for as many years as our nation has lived, countless brave people have given their lives for it so that we might pursue happiness and safety in peace and live our lives knowing that document keeps at bay the darkest of times.

But it seems, at least by the unhappiness of so many, that we are up against that wall of the darkest of times. Even I catch myself being annoyed at someone who is happy. We all wish to do something to show we really are the kind of citizens who will stand up to confront injustice and fraud and greed and rampant political lunacy, but we find ourselves caught in this weird void of paralysis, feeling helpless even as our humanity is assaulted and our basic constitutional rights are dragged through the debris and rubble left behind by those in power. And being in such a state, the average citizen becomes cynical.

I understand. I keep wavering, going to that place of merciless desperation, that "what are we going to do" thinking, to "hell yes we can execute our god-given intelligence and deal with this," my yo-yoing there and back somersaults me in high-anxiety stress, landing me in a place where all I can sometimes do is exist in a perennial state of hand-wringing worry. But for my children, my friends, and my community, for the future of my society and all those other members of my global community, I keep searching for an answer.

It seems, however, that rather than do the hard work of finding solutions through trial and error and a lot of energy, as shown by the recent popularity of those unprincipled louts now running the country, inhabiting our sacred government sanctums, many people would rather blame, scapegoat, and perjure immigrants with making false accusations against them, assailing not only their intent and questioning their motives but instilling fear in Americans that immigrants are the harbingers of Armageddon.

It's laughable to consider for even a second that any sane person would believe that immigrants and refugees are the reason for America's problems. Right-wing ideologues can turn an otherwise pleasant day into a festering toothache for their opponents. And the really mean ones rip babies away from their mothers. Put innocent women in cages. Deport asylum seekers to their certain deaths. In short, practice every sinister tactic available, all of it contrary to our democracy.

And since I don't like being mean and it's against my basic principles as a human to prey on the helpless, how did I overcome my sense of painful helplessness? The solution was easily within reach but it relied heavily on my deciding to use my own American-educated, inspired judgment and not swim mindlessly into the herring net of the mob: I offered a job to a refugee.

His name was Sae-Po, Burmese, with three daughters and two boys and a wife, and one night while they slept in their village in Myanmar/Burma, vigilantes hunting Christian believers were going house to house setting fire to each and killing the inhabitants. Sae-Po barely escaped, and for the next fifteen years he and his family somehow survived in a refugee camp situated between Burma and Vietnam.

When I met him, he got off the bus, leading his sixteen-year-old daughter by the hand. She had been severely assaulted by the marauders and seemed sunken in a deep mystic-hole in herself where she found safety in her isolation. Sae-Po was so kind to her.

I have two daughters and can't imagine anything happening to them, but to Sae-Po, I swear, I don't how, but he smiled at me, bowed, and had the most benign and gracious composure I'd ever seen. I was in the presence of someone special.

———

I'd been driving down the road when Catholic Charity Services announced on the radio they needed sponsors, and right then I drove to their office and signed up and the next day met Sae-Po. I'd helped refugees before. In the mid '90s, when I had my Black Mesa farm, I opened it to refugees fleeing South American tyrants and Mexican drug lords from Central America, and I had them use my place as a recharging station—we let them rest, gave them fresh clothing, food, supplies for the journey north, and sent them on their way, waving and hugging and even crying sometimes.

I was in my late thirties and I was radical to the bone, did pretty much what a poet does, that is, read a lot of poets—Neruda, Mistral, Che, Lincoln, Mother Jones, Lorca—and got inspired by them to act in ways that benefited humanity. When it came to deciding what was just, and since I had my own experience as a Chicano to reflect on and make decisions, I felt pretty good about helping people. There'd been many times in my life when police and drug lords terrorized our barrios and pulled people out of their homes, took whatever they wanted, and threatened to return if we said anything.

I spent eleven years in an orphanage, and when I ran away for the last time to avoid being sent to Boys Town, I lived on the streets, and without good people helping me, offering me a meal and a bed and a smile, I'd be dead.

Sae-Po and I began to work together at my farm north of Santa Fe, New Mexico. I was building a cabin. I gave him my hunter's trailer to live in. He'd stay five days, and then I'd drop him off at his apartment in Albuquerque, give him a few days to rest, pick him up, and we go at it again. I saw him lift boulders twice his size, doing this all day, saw him shovel and saw and nail and carry and wheelbarrow and climb and install and sweep and clean and never stop. He would not use an inside bathroom; he went out to the forest. After a day's work, he would wash in the creek and put on his robe, and we would sit in the cabin and eat. Oftentimes, no, all the time I was so messed up from the day's labor, I threw myself on the floor and slept. On one occasion, Sae-Po asked me to take off my shirt and turn over on my stomach. He then stepped bare-footed on my back, and I swear, within minutes of his toes and heels pinching and pressing against my muscles, the pain and aches were gone. I was amazed and asked where he learned that, and he said it was one way he made ends meet in the refugee camp he'd lived in for years.

I told him, "Dude, you got serious shit going on there, homie. I mean, damn, dude, not even all these so-called Santa Fe master masseurs in a year get even close to what you can do in a few minutes." All he did was smile and bow, and I swear, I loved him so much that moment, loved what he was teaching me about life.

We spoke mostly in nods and gestures and smiles and pointing to things. I told him I'd like to give him some acres to work; he could have them, a gift from me to him. It was obvious he loved farming, and sometimes he would try to tell me things, like how if he had his best friend from the refugee camp with him, a Vietnamese, they would make the best farm in America. His eyes lit up, his body seemed to grow an aura of joy in its stillness, his head nodded up and down, farm love . . . farm best . . . and it was so sweet and sad at the same time. My heart broke as I knew I was sitting next to someone, all five foot one inches of this giant, who, I knew with absolute certainty, was by far the best farmer on the continent, and I knew, given a chance, his farm would be beautiful.

But when I went to pick him up one day at his apartment, I was informed by his neighbor tenants that he had been picked up in the middle of the night and led out of his apartment, along with his wife and kids, all of them in plastic handcuffs. I know he went without a fight, his concern more on his family.

Sae-Po loved the hunter's trailer so much I gave it to him, but it's still there, sitting in the field. And soon after that is when I started the poem "When I Walk Through

That Door, I Am," because he changed my life, and I know that wherever he is, he is still spreading joy and comradery and giving of himself to create in people and places a joining of equal souls in harmony and pursuit of true democratic values.

———

Everything we know about them is wrong and yet they come at just the right moment in time, to define for us what Democracy is; in this blue, white, and red scarf of time, this silk, cotton, and wool scarf that blows like northern lights across the sky, and our eyes that look at the horizon wondering who we are and who we are becoming, laboring under our biases and fears and laziness and greed; we got them all wrong.

They come giving, not taking. They create community. They believe in justice. They seek peace. How much more simple can that get for our muddle-brained minions who create insane immigration policies? Refugees enrich, not deplete, they imagine and create places, not impose inglorious eyesores on our landscapes, they welcome not spurn, they feed not starve, they work not cheat, they earn not take.

They come to repair our democracy, to lay the patient on the table and carefully apply the sutures, cut out the cancer of cynicism and sew up the wound, disinfect and pray over the wound, attend to the patient, feed it, lift its head and give it water and sing to it and keep it warm and safe, even as the patient screams and swings wildly at them with knives and guns, drags them away in maddened fits of rage, and locks them in dark dungeons or in cages and starves and beats them and even rapes them, they wait patiently, hoping for a time when the patient tires and returns to its sanity.

I went it alone after that, decided to do the work myself without help. I spent a good deal of time hiking forest trails. I sat alone on rocks and each evening sat on the couch staring at the fireplace flames, imagining Sae-Po was sitting next to me, remembering our shared meals, his toe-n-heel massages. There was no obstacle he wouldn't take on, and when I was absolutely exhausted, his encouraging smile always came at an opportune time to help me continue working. He weighed perhaps a hundred pounds at most. I offered all kinds of food, but he ate only rice and beans and he loved my tortillas so much I taught him how to make them. His only triumph came when he handed over his pay to his wife to buy groceries and pay the rent and get medicine for their daughter. I couldn't understand this man, who had been shamed and burned out and spit at and humiliated in a thousand different ways, and yet all he offered was acceptance and patience and guidance. He didn't want to be rich; he wanted to be at peace, for his kids to have opportunity and a decent education. He made so much out of so little.

———

As a way of dealing with my own sadness and grief, I walked a lot and started writing little lines down. With each day, more and more asylum seekers were being imprisoned, their children torn from their arms, men dragged from homes, children beaten by INS, women raped as regularly and commonly as if the rapists had been trained in military and police academies, that it was normal and expected, part of the policy and procedure.

I remembered how Sae-Po loved the rain, how he missed his country Burma with such huge sadness that when he mentioned it, the word imbued his features with a veil of excruciating loneliness. I remember how careful he was to eat every morsel of rice; every meal he cleaned his plate of every rice grain and bean with a piece of tortilla, and then he washed his plate. He was always courteous and grateful. The pine tree enchanted him. The boulders were his friends; he would caress them with his fingers and say, "Oooo," as if the rock had consciousness and was aware of the caresses. He wore sandals but never wore them in the cabin, he liked green fields and grass and the creek water flowing over the creek stones, he loved the sunlight and sun, and basked in hard work, he mired himself in silence, almost never talking, and I guess if this poem is anything, it is a tribute to him and thousands like him, who I owe so much to for teaching me how to be a better man and appreciate what I have—mostly my family.

And he gave me the courage to do something, to do what I could. Although it is never enough, I no longer wring my hands in worry. I act, I engage, and I write.

Jimmy Santiago Baca is the author of *A Place to Stand*, which was adapted into a documentary film. He is also the author of *Martín & Meditations on the South Valley*, winner of the American Book Award, and *Working in the Dark*, winner of the Southwest Book Award, and he is the writer and executive producer of *Blood In/Blood Out*, a Hollywood Pictures feature that has gained a cult following of millions globally. His book *Healing Earthquakes* was an honoree of the Phi Beta Kappa Society and the recipient of a Pushcart Prize, the Hispanic Heritage Award for Literature, and the Cornelius P. Turner Award, which honors GED graduates who have made "outstanding contributions" in the areas of education, justice, and social welfare. He was honored with the Humanitarian Award from Albuquerque and has held many Chairs of

Distinction, including the Endowed Hulbert Chair, Colorado College; the Wallace Stevens Chair, Yale; and the Regents Chair, University of California at Berkeley. He was also a Barnes and Noble Discover author. After writing a Mexican *Roots* series for HBO, he established his nonprofit, Cedar Tree, Inc., and produced two documentaries, *Lost Voices* and *Moving the River Back Home*. Cedar Tree continues to grow and assist communities through its bookmobile, which supplies free books to libraries and schools on reservations, in barrios, and in inner-city educational centers. The organization also sends interns to assist teachers in rural communities lacking educational resources. For his work teaching thousands of adults and kids to read and write, the University of New Mexico awarded him an honorary PhD. While continuing to write, he facilitates writing workshops worldwide, visiting dozens of prisons, youth offender facilities, and alternative schools for at-risk youth annually, in as many countries. He's the author of eighteen books of poetry, fiction, and nonfiction, all in print.